THE NATIONAL
POETRY SERIES

The National Poetry Series was established in 1978 to ensure the publication of five books annually through participating publishers. Publication is funded by the late James A. Michener, the Copernicus Society of America, Edward J. Piszek, the Lannan Foundation, and the National Endowment for the Arts.

2000
COMPETITION WINNERS

Susan Atefat-Peckham of Michigan
That Kind of Sleep

Jean Donnelly of Washington, DC
Anthem

Spencer Short of Iowa
Tremolo

Rebecca Wolff of New York
Manderley

Susan Wood of Texas
Asunder

That Kind of Sleep

That Kind of Sleep

Susan Atefat-Peckham

COFFEE HOUSE PRESS
Minneapolis

2001

COFFEE HOUSE PRESS is an independent nonprofit literary publisher supported in part by a grant provided by the Minnesota State Arts Board, through an appropriation by the Minnesota State Legislature and the National Endowment for the Arts. Support has also been provided by Elmer L. & Eleanor J. Andersen Foundation; Athwin Foundation; the Bush Foundation; Patrick and Aimee Butler Family Foundation; Historical Remedies; Honeywell Foundation; Lila Wallace-Reader's Digest Fund; McKnight Foundation; The St. Paul Companies, Inc. Foundation; the law firm of Schwegman, Lundberg, Woessner & Kluth, P.A.; the Target Foundation; West Group; and many individual donors. To you and our many readers across the country, we send our thanks for your continuing support.

COFFEE HOUSE PRESS books are available to the trade through our primary distributor, Consortium Book Sales & Distribution, 1045 Westgate Drive, Saint Paul, MN 55114. For personal orders, catalogs, or other information, write to: Coffee House Press, 27 North Fourth Street, Suite 400, Minneapolis, MN 55401.

Good books are brewing at coffeehousepress.org.

LIBRARY OF CONGRESS CIP INFORMATION

Atefat-Peckham, Susan, 1970-
    That kind of sleep : poetry / by Susan Atefat-Peckham.
      p. cm.
    ISBN 1-56689-116-7 (alk. paper)
    1. Women--Iran--Poetry. 2. Iran--Poetry. I. Title.
PS3616.E28 T48 2001
811'.6--DC21

2001032480

My thanks to all writers and friends who have supported these poems with kind words and generosity, especially primary readers Joel Peckham, Hilda Raz, and Ted Kooser.

My affectionate gratitude to my loving parents, continually, the light at my side, to Joel, Cyrus, and Darius—all inspirations.

for my family

    who teach
me how to speak
from love

for my children

    who dream
this world, love
Mother

Acknowledgments

I am grateful to the editors of the following publications,
where these poems, some in slightly different form, first appeared:

Magazines

Borderlands—Texas Poetry Review: "At Noon" and "What Everyone Does"

International Quarterly: "Dreaming of a Dancer" and "Gold"

The MacGuffin: "*Arouss*—Bride," "Ironing the Staten Island Ferry,"
and "Mosaic Women"

Northwest Review: "A Karaj Boy," "At the Palace Garden,"
"At the Streetcorner," and "Trying to Leave"

Onthebus: "*Boro!*—Get Away!" and "To the House"

Prairie Schooner: "*Marvari*—The Pearl Tree," "Remembering the Weaver,"
"Grandmother's Prayer," "When One Has Filled with Face,"
"Nina's Dance," and "For Tradition"

Puerto Del Sol: "Dates"

The Southern Poetry Review: "At Exactly Two"

The Sycamore Review: "*Ameh Joon*—Aunt Dear"

The Texas Review: "Stoning Soheila"

Anthology

Common Ground: An Anthology of Multi-cultural Writing (Prentice Hall),
"Avenue Vali Asr," "Pahlavi Street," and "Remembering the Weaver"

Jelaluddin Rumi is quoted from *The Essential Rumi*,
as translated by Coleman Barks and John Moyne(Castlebooks, 1997).

CONTENTS

～ I ～

～ II ～

If anyone asks you
how the perfect satisfaction
of all our sexual wanting
will look, lift your face
and say,

>   *Like this.*

When someone mentions the gracefulness
of the nightsky, climb up on the roof
and dance and say,

>   *Like this?*

If anyone wants to know what "spirit" is,
or what "God's fragrance" means,
lean your head toward him or her.
Keep your face there close.

>   *Like this.*

—RUMI

Marvari
THE PEARL TREE

—for Joel

He asks if I remember them—I remember
few, I say. Leaning deep into leaves,
my uncle pinched and turned white berries
from the pearl tree in hands as old and twisted
as the branches. He rushed to where I waited,
uncurled his palm and tossed them, rolling
into linen spread on my lap. He squeezed
my fingers into his and pushed the silver point
through each fruit, tugging on the thread
until my palms were wet with juice.

I feel the grip and weight of a white necklace
soft and warm in the curve of my neck. I return
to the garden, alive again with yellow flowers
and the fresh scent of cucumbers. I am tall
enough now, but he holds my fingers back
and thrusts his own arthritic hand in leaves,
his mind fixed on a memory. One wet finger
unfolds and reveals a palmful of pearls.
He asks if I remember him.

Remembering the Weaver

My uncle points a shriveled finger
at a weaver rocking in silk shadows,
lost in the hard smell of old clothes
and cracked wood. He asks if I know
the quiet place where fingers pluck
the strings like harpists, their blue veins
webbing like young roots, gathering
bones. Her eyes wrinkle the pattern
her hands design to knot her life

in the loom. Come girl! he said.
Come! Then he thrust me into noise,
stumbling through the woolly tufts
of red and yellow where fingers
twitched and feet dropped at multi-
colored walls. I know the dark spot
where once I crawled under strung
wood to tickle dirty toes. I hear quick
threads unravel. The children

are gone, the echo of their voices
muffled in spools, and she weaves from
somewhere under her chador, a black knot
hanging from the great loom, pulling
threads till the last strand of her name is tied
and cut. I think she knows I tickled her
once. I leave her a coin for her trouble,
then gather my uncle's fingers to tell him
I remember only the tall shadows of looms.

Grandmother's Prayer

When one is accepted into the Muslim faith,
it is traditional to also choose a Muslim name.

I bent to the stone and touched my forehead
to its sharp edge. The rug smelled of must
and rain. I wondered if Grandmother watched.
She always stood against the light, a dark
glow at the morning window, her silhouette,
a black pillar at the curtain, her hand hanging
white and clean, and how could I

forget her pointing to the kabob sizzling
on the irons, and she looking to me as if
to say it was all right for me to pick the meat
from coals and taste the hot, grilled
flesh.
       I wanted to do myself some honor
and choose my own god. There is some
honor in not believing everything they say.
There is some honor in keeping one's name.

I lift my head from the cold beige stone,
chipped and heavy, the beads snaking
over and around the prayer rug, over
and around the stone and pray, *Allah
hu Akbar, Allah hu Akbar,* seeing her blink
approvingly from the light, hearing the noise
of a language foreign to our native land.

When One Has Filled with Face

—*for Naneh Jan*
Imitation is the greatest form of flattery

                                        Porr Rou!
Grandfather said, his voice glazed gray as he
slammed close the bathroom window. Meaning
Naneh Jan was Full of Face, not me. My face
was full of my tongue, of knowing I chased her
around and around the roses, my back hooked
to her crooked shadow, my voice twisted to her
jagged noises, for hours. Dry ground pulled
water from the garden hose she held, spotting
my ankles, her toes—my face was filled
with knowing.

                              Later my face
knew it earned her wrinkled glare, her sun-baked
finger sharpening at the knot in my shadow
as if it pointed at some now-past space we just
emptied. In the house, I swung the window open
to the upward thrust of her hands, water, face
grinning through a spray as the glass and tiles filled
with sunlit drops arching their backs from her

fingers like a thousand silver coins. Grandfather
woke from the spill inside—*Porr Rou!*
he said at last.

              And led me by his hand
where I dried, where I watched the old woman's
face fill with the noons of my absence, with silent
spaces left behind, once I went back to America.
Outside in roses, her shadow leaned to a dry future
where she would die before I returned. I watched
her stand in that kind of present, a future sharpening
the past, stood with Grandfather, shivering the years
I would carry the quiet of a window still dripping,
of water striping the tiles, her ancient form smiling,
a half-coin, behind the beveled light.

Arouss
BRIDE

Balancing on my toes, I pushed
my arms up petticoats, squinted
at my face, round in the silver
curves of the samovar. Lili looped
buttons into a line hanging neat
and loose like strung beads.

Grandfather sat waiting with string,
netting lace around his fingers,
waited for me to come and finish
our game but dropped the string
and slapped his knees, yelling
Arouss! Arouss! Bride! Bride!

We left. He should have come
with us. Instead, he pulled my fist
as if a thread through eyes of stiff
bracelets, said, Yes, Yes, we will,
sometime, to visit, your Grandma
and I, Happy Birthday, for now.

I blew the candles cold, one wish
burnt and lost in warmth, saying,
Have to leave to America now,
can't stay to hear you sing sad
verses, Sadi, Hafiz, Rumi,
can't stay to pull you through

smoke of burning corn, through
sun-dried streets of bazaar
peasants. His gold still rounds
my wrist like old, half-forgotten
words, whispering *Arouss, Arouss,
Arouss.* And I will marry soon.

NINA'S DANCE

They said she never would,
and she said no at first, tipping
her wide neck, her face red
and bashful, her pear-shaped
body standing quiet and uneasy
at the center of the room.

I thought of how I once played
at her glass cabinet crowded
with figurines. She always wanted us
to bring her something back, something
to care for, something to hold and own.
Grandfather wouldn't put her away.
You know why, he would say—
I fear God. Enough to keep her home.

She stared for a moment, then
bobbed in strained jerks to the violin
and tambourines, her round
belly bouncing, her stockings
unrolled to the hem of her skirt.
She spread her stiff arms, hooked
her wrists. Her eyes filled dark.
Her hips curled sounds, her hair
rounded to flushed circles of cheek.
She bent her knees to the clapping,
awkward and ecstatic.

Chehel Setoun
FORTY COLUMNS

—for Father

Boys sit in rows like fledgling pigeons between
and among the twenty columns, between

and among the twenty columns, scribbling
in their writing pads, seeing themselves fade

in the narrow pool out front. One ten year old
finishes early, leans his shaved head and cupped

ears against the wood, stares up into the mirrored
dome and sees a place away from columns and dry

heat, dreams of my Uncle Atcfat's words and books.
And Ameh pawns her jewelry for him to travel far.

I love him best of all, Father said, and poured
another gallon of New Jersey humidity from the tank.

Water filled the grass. I almost heard Uncle Atefat sing
Hafiz to me. How he led me past the roses, past fountains

in his yard, under a canopy, and sat cross-legged
on pillows lining the carpets. And in cool seclusion,

pulled his books for me, even if I were to be a woman.
My fingers drifted slow along the cracked bindings,

stitches at their centers. Even if I were to be a woman,
he believed. There are only five of us left, Father

would say. Then back to labor over world economy
at his American desk. Father pulls me fast and forward

through his Isfahan childhood, hot streets
and dust of bazaars. He brings me here.

Another old palace, I think. I stuff my hands
in my pockets and finger the piece of gazz

he gave me, hot and stuck to the stitched seam.
And Mother's eyes rest on memories.

Uncle Atefat is now a wrinkled man and smaller
than I had remembered, lost somewhere

in cigarette smoke at a family reunion. He sings.
Been away too long, he says of me. She doesn't

understand the words, he says. Doesn't understand.
I stand under the mirrored dome, look into its rounds

almost able to see my soul a thousand times itself, my
father's eye a thousand times the center. He walks

to one column not expecting dried memory of wood.
I turn to see him stand, arms folded, king-like, saying,

It's here. Right here. As a boy. I sat here for my test,
then told me his immigrant dreams of America. He looks

to wood as if it might remember cupped ears. We stand
between and among the columns, cracked and tall.

Twenty-two ripple with silver. My fingers touch still
water, rippling, again, again, again, circling what I love.

NOTE: "The Chehel Setoun Palace place of forty columns is one of the
monuments which has been constructed in the Jahan Namma Garden in
the reign of Shah Abbas I. The palace is so called because twenty
wooden columns of the frontal terrace are reflected in the pool which is
in front of the monument making forty columns. On the other hand in
Iranian literature the number forty is used to denote any large number.
[It] was renovated with mirror decoration in Safavid era and as a result
the mirror ornamentation period was begun." (Copied from a handwrit-
ten sign outside the palace doors.)

FOR TRADITION

I struggled with my grandmother's rosebush,
pinching and bending branches, picking
each red and yellow petal from tender
stems. I pushed them into a glass of water
set on the cement ledge and waited patiently
in her lap, lacing my inked fingers around
her neck, stroking the flushed skin, watching
the black calluses on a soldier's hands
through a space in the gate and wondered
if his twitching fingers could reach the glass.

I now see the deep lines in her forehead,
and a whispered prayer plays on her wrinkled
lips. She holds the Koran to my swelling mouth
waiting for me, a woman now, to kiss the ruffled
pages and pass under its broken spine. I hear
her, full with care, spill the water at the gate
and drop warm petals, For tradition, she says,
for my quick return, as if the trail smeared
in the mortar behind the car made a difference,
as if a kiss on the holy book would keep us safe.

GOLD

—for Grandmother

It hung from her
throat, its chains falling to baked seeds,
to yellow stains of saffron under her nails,
the sweet scent on her thumb as she held
and kissed my face. And when the sunlight
sang in her arms at noon, she showed me
how she rocked my shadow to sleep.
Time creates a space far from where
our shadows stay.

Mother used to say
there was no better way to receive a gift.
The war pretended to give—nuts and seeds
packed with smuggled grains of gold. Still
she always used to say that, the mornings
the brown package came. Grandmother
pulled the nuts loose. And pushing from
pistachio shells and watermelon seeds, gold
spilled from the hollow of a shell.

Emptied shells
seem like earth stones wrapped in her prayer
rug. And Tehran sets its gold behind
its roofs and domes. In the sky, her voice
lulls its head, the number of times she calls
me down to bed softens, my name rising
stairs along the east wall, rising to the roof
like candlelight. At sunrise, light sways
along my face like time, like age, like place.

IRONING THE
STATEN ISLAND FERRY

The silver hull still presses its water
into the port, settling its body, tight
and rounded, into the Hudson bay.
My chadored grandmother couldn't
have done it better herself on our couch.
How her laughter curls. But I've
already forgotten too much. How I
squeezed her tight when the steel doors
rose and the hull dropped to a wet
swirling rush, held her again in a dried
Tehran alley outside her gates.
Grandfather's bowl of water set
for us, spilled in the road as tradition
would have its water squeezed red
with dust and pushed into the gutter.
Mother still says, Go wash your face
and hands, And come out like a lady,
Barikalla, Good girl, if I cry.

While her pins waited between her
teeth, waist bent to the board, Mother
pushed the hot metal to waxed paper
and leaves. Steam wrinkled past
her face like Grandmother's chadored
kisses. Her hands fanned the wood
like layered sky, her fingers, sweet
with red leaves, rubbed the rain hot.
But time juts Mother's lip out
at the bottom. My hands are filled
with her pins. Her fingers wipe her
brow, folded like Grandmother's lips.
I press my words, press that old Ferry
rumbling its space in my past, a silver
crease, a sharp alley, spilt water,
blistered spots of red.

Autumn Letter

—for Mother

Mother always had her way
with words, squinting at my page
to find herself, to catch my foreign
breath and let it linger, see it blister
in lines and die a full death. Ey,
she said when I teased her
for the hours she would spend,
for calling the flower, Gerumium,
for the way she spelled, Esnickar,
Ey, she said, *Na Cun*. And *she*
once corrected *my* English.

Dying trees stretch their bones
up and forward like hungry men,
the red spreading top-first, the wet
falling. Her broken words leave
traces in iced fossils of leaves,
her drying body in a rose
I clipped with the blunt tip
of my thumb.

I gather leaves
with my husband, saying, I need
a red one, or, I need the one
that has no tears. Now they crunch
in pages of Khayyám. I think
of the letter I just read with words
cut out and rewritten. Circled above,
then scribbled, *Daddy says like this.*

She says a letter makes its way
to me. She says I ought to see
what words she's spelled this time.
I won't tell her what I write, but she
asks. Snow crowds a windowpane.
Frost blooms and fingers names.
Nebraska wind cuts quick. I've moved
geraniums in for winter. My aching
bones long for mother's words,
dried earth, blistered lines of green.

~ II ~

When lovers moan,
they're telling our story.

Like this.

I am a sky where spirits live.
Stare into this deepening blue,
while the breeze says a secret.

Like this.

When someone asks what there is to do,
light the candle in his hand.

Like this.

—RUMI

Pahlavi Street

She was just fourteen when she sneaked
down Pahlavi street. No one ever knew.
The doctor sewed her back together
so her father could smile at her suitors
and say "Yes, she is a virgin."

She tucked that lock of hair away from
her sweaty brow and under the silk, but
the postar already saw. He pushed her down,
his heel at the arch of her back, her body
writhing and curled, and spanked her hard.

She wraps and rewraps her crooked shape,
her dirty, old palm upward, waiting for
the sound of clinking coins or the crunch
of a folded bill, waiting for the children
to offer her nuts or candy.

She begs with the smoldering eyes
of a storyteller, twisting her mouth behind
the black cloth to hide words from the postars,
curling around herself, pink and tender, selling
her life to the children on Pahlavi Street.

Avenue Vali Asr

—for Kholeh Lili

We need another Rosa Parks
to pin herself to that front seat
and say, I am too old for later.

Smoke folded edges in city air.
Buses littered streets, dented, worn,
old tin cans crushed at the station.

I unstuck the front doors, pushed
the edges forward and apart to meet
the fat thumb pointing backward.

Boro Ounja! he said. Over there!
And I turned to see my place
among the colored scarves behind.

My breasts warmed steel rounds
at my ribs. I was half-sick of standing
there, breathing in wet wool

of hair, breathing in their breaths.
We are not sheep, I said, We are not
sheep. A woman turned. I tugged

at clinging cloth. Someone shushed
me quiet. Do not speak, she said,
It is good this way, without voice.

She dabbed her head and sweat pressed
through colored silk. She pushed
and shoved the heat for space.

I saw her hand grip at the window.
I heard the bustle of a large woman
behind me telling the others to hear

and peasants lolled in their chairs
up front, sunned their hairy hands
under the smoke of windows, kicked

their feet up on empty chairs, leering
into the small noises we made.
I know that words can't help them here.

Hot breath hovers in old wind.
A folded sky spreads in Tehran.

Grandmother's Bag of Earth

Her face smelled of dill and saffron,
skin as sweet and tanned, fingers dyed
from kneading meat. The drawstring
on her bag of earth pulls tight in her
closet, where Grandfather keeps
his wedding shoes still polished new
fifty-three years on the shelf. They say
they each have separate spaces. He gets
the sky. She gets what's pulled woolen
under her chador.
              Aging, she gives
Mother her photographs, her terrmeh,
her samovar, the bag of earth she opened
once, laid flat and patted her palms on,
chalked her face so she could pray
even if she were maimed and dying.
God never forgets when it's time
to pray.

Once rooted in chopped beef
and blood, her hands now dry like dust.
Her eyes once gleamed like almonds.
Mother pulls the drawstring tight, closes
the closet door. The moon lifts the wind
with honeysuckle, moving barefoot
on the roof, around her clotheslines,
its head bare under the black Tehran sky.

To the House

I should have emptied my colander of rice
into their smiling eyes, rice so fresh that saltwater
steamed and dripped on my sandaled toes. Postars'
eyes lingered on little girls when they passed,
pretending not to watch from shadows.

A screech and halt and they dragged shrouded
women under by the necks of their scarves, stuffed
in a postar's car and branded whores because of one
button missing on a coat, shoved under the roof
like cargo, one by one, some struggling, some passive,
all hauled to the station to stand before a judge
who decided the proper exchange of coins for whippings.

My mother unknotted her scarf, pulled the burning
cigarette from her smoking lips, and pressed
my fingers around the cracked lipstick
marks of its moist, tan rim, whispering
"You want to try it? Try it—"

Fariba's Daughters

*Iranian law states that once a girl turns nine, she
is of age and must wear the chador in public places.*

Fariba pulls her scarf off when we are alone,
holds her head taut like a winter oak, dark
and bare. She likes her books under
the mattress, under the wooded tucking
of blankets, between mattress and box spring.
She asks me if it's good to read, and reaches
under white to pull the book from its hiding.

I hear her voice, clear and strong, talking
of school, asking how freedom feels,
asking if I had sex before marriage like girls
in the West, or if I was a good Iranian virgin.
I tell her what freedom is. It is noon
and the prayers outside are loud. I ask her
why she never teaches her daughters
a different way. Her stare is hard. Almost
as hard as the roll of her eyes when someone
wants more doukgh, more bakhlava.
She is worn from wanting.

This is my favorite—Jean Paul Sartre, they say
his wife was smart, she says. But I can see her
daughter Attar turning with the scarf, winding it
around her head and loving to see herself as her
mother in the dresser mirror. I ask Fariba why
she wears it. For my daughters, her fingers
catch in her hair, for my daughters.

I remember when Father said I wasn't to wear
a chador to the bazaar. I was not old enough
to choose my way, that I would be safe.
So Grandmother pulled me under her chador,
wove me into her folds, just me and her under
cloth so postars would leave us alone. *Bepau,*
she said, Watch it. And I thought it was fun
and safe and soft standing against Grandmother's
lap, seeing from an opening near her hands.
Perhaps there is some joy in being captive,
some comfort in knowing we obey.

Nebraska winter drops in tufts. Does Sartre
still hide in wood? What does Fariba read
today? Attar turning, almost nine. What color
will her first scarf be? Woolen snow drifts
and weaves its way. Daughters are warm
wrapped in their Grandmothers' chadors.

Mosaic Women

I know the hard smell of dust
and hot tar on flat Middle-Eastern
roofs. I hopped barefoot up
the cement stairs that climbed
to the roof of your house
and, swinging from a clothes line,
heard the hovering voice of a man
singing prayers from the slender
forms of minarets and bulging
turquoise domes. I often stared
at her from there, the mosaic
woman fixed on the palace
wall, four hundred years old,
her clay eyes cracked and ancient.
When it was time to pray at dawn
I saw you wrap yourself in flowers,
watch me and whisper, bend
to a stone called earth, teach
me as you counted the beads
on an old string unfolded
in the silk of a colored carpet.

I know the crawling ants
that speckled your porch
with brown at noon. While
you slept I fed them nuts
and watched soldiers stand.
I heard those noises crack
through sun-beaten streets
and never knew why Grandpa
turned out all the lamps at night
and lit the candles, why they lined
the streets outside your house
in single file, why women in black
sheets, silent and brooding,
shuffled past the palace wall,
never looking at those hips,
round and wide, that mouth, red
and full, that hair, black and loose.

I know the warm scent of wrinkled
hands, old and knotted, tending
roses and honeysuckle. I played
house with the copper dishes you
gave and wore your wedding dress,
dipped my fingers black in the jam
you made, smeared your wrinkles
red. At night I heard them call
you from the minarets again
and saw your aged and tired
eyes blink between the flowers
of your chador as you bent
and whispered, bent and whispered,
pushed another turquoise bead
along the raspy string with each
refrain. I pulled aside the white
veils of my bed, and knew
the moonlit mosque at my window,
the gold silhouette of a crescent
moon rising from the dome, dark
and still, against a mosaic woman.

WHEN SHE WAS NINE

Muslims open the Koran at random when there is
a marriage. If the page opened is good, the union
is blessed and a goat is sacrificed at the threshold.

They told her it was good, the mullah
flipping the dusty pages of his holy book
looking for God's approval in the yellowing words.
The Koran opened on a good page, so when she
was nine she slumped in her wedding dress,
half a woman, the swellings of her breasts
not quite swellings yet. Barely listening
to that man chanting from his heavy book,
she stood on a crotchety stool, still not as tall
as her old husband, her feet groping the wooden
edges, afraid of falling. She cried under the white net
of her wedding veil over the slaughtered goat
at her threshold, the blood staining its hairy throat,
trickling hot streams into the soil for her good
fortune. All around her people turned and people
danced, music played. When she was nine
she married him, balancing on a stool, the steam
rising and curling around the bleeding animal.

CANDLEMAKER

Her eager form leans into heat,
her back arched over the pans,
her arms stirring. She rolls
the burning red into the soft folds
of her hands, shaping it to her flesh
and bones, trying to forget her husband's
eyes when he wanted to try again.

Her hard stare rests on kneaded forms
ridged with fingerprints, and she remembers
him cupping the broken petals in his palms,
the shards of wax still tumbling on
the checkered floor. Her callused
hands hover over the pans, red
and impatient, mending, forgetting.

Shadows play on her breasts when she
leans over the flame. He watches her
busy fingers and wonders if she loves
him yet. She twists the wick in tight turns,
pointing its frayed threads, thinking of candles,
and sculpting, and dying flowers, feeling
his eyes, wondering why he watches.

STONING SOHEILA

Shut in hot walls and thatched roofs
of mountains, they drove Soheila into cool
ground, wound in ropes at the foot
of the mountain, her head sticking white
and silent from red dust like a desert
bloom, and she remembers when she
was ten and tore a kite, squatting for hours
in the desert heat over wood and string,
rubbing her fingers raw on the knots.
She worked in the city for cloth, bowed
her head to an eager master and begged
him to forgive her when the tea boiled
over the samovar. Summoned to his room,
the same each day his wife was gone,
she felt his hairy hands skip, fat and slow,
along the buttons. He gave pistachios
and dates for thanks and she said nothing.

Some cows, some land, some rugs
for her beauty, and Zohreh worked all day,
her hand black with kohl and henna.
She slid her turquoise pendant down
the gold and hung it in Soheila's hair,
a drop of the Caspian on her forehead.
We are family, the old woman said,
and wrapped her niece in the silk
and silver weave of her best chador.
Soheila was washed and left with her
husband that night, and she said nothing.

She bore her husband nine children.
He preferred American cars and sex
with city whores, to beat open the door
with flailing arms and heavy fists.
She hurried down the winding streets
bloodied with her youngest, limp
in her arms, sneaked to her childhood
home and found her father in black
weeping into her mother's necklace.
He kissed her hand, There is nothing
for you here, and sent her back.

Her husband followed when she carried
dinners to a widower's house, heard
her sing his children to sleep. Sick
with rage, he chased her down the street
with stones and screamed, Adulterer!
Whore! Shameless One! And Soheila
said nothing. Allah protect and keep
you from the Law, Zohreh whispered,
then buttoned Soheila in her finest dress,
its white skirts yellowed and creased
by the hard corners of an old drawer.

She watches the man dressed like a cleric
strut the only village street like a messiah,
remembers how he sat on her couch smacking
his lips, Soheila, you are so deserving—
I can visit you now and then? Stones beat
her head as if it were a pillar of Shayton,
as if the tiny mound in the dry earth
were Mount Arafat moved from Mecca,
now towering here. Zohreh remembers
the morning Soheila was born, wrapped
in a linen bundle and named for the star,
and dreams of digging the piles of rocks
to find that quiet face. Crazy and mumbling,
she carries her linen and kneels in the sun
of the village square, scratching the stone,
searching the dust with knotted fingers
for something to wrap, to carry home.

~ III ~

When someone quotes the old poetic image
about clouds gradually uncovering the moon,
slowly loosen knot by knot the strings
of your robe.
          Like this?

If anyone wonders how Jesus raised the dead,
don't try to explain the miracle.
Kiss me on the lips.
                    Like this. Like this.

When someone asks what it means
to "die for love," point
                    here.

If someone asks how tall I am, frown
and measure with your fingers the space
between the creases on your forehead.
                              This tall.

The soul sometimes leaves the body, then returns.
When someone doesn't believe that,
walk back into my house.
                    Like this.

—RUMI

DATES

Three days and they wrapped
his washed body in muslin,
no lumbering sounds of coffins
carried, only the white ripple
of cloth. I sat back where all
women sat, staring from behind
a wooden net, carved and set
aside. The others swayed
as if crows under the mirrored
dome of the mosque webbed
in their chadors, breathing cloth
in and out of their wailing,
in and out. Their black heads
bobbed against the carved light
of the wooden boundary, the roar
and echo of men beating themselves
downstairs, pounding their chests
tightly, fists on flesh, to the rhythm
of a prayer for the dead.

A woman stood and held a tray,
the edges of her chador clenched
in her teeth and wrapped so tightly
around her face that it cut angles
into her cheeks. She offered us
a silver tray of fruit as chanting
grew, beating grew, that fleshy
rhythm. And the woman
with dates walked the aisles
offering the shriveled skin
and its sweet stench on a silver tray,
making her way from one woman
to the next. Somewhere under
Iranian earth, seamless cloth lay
on its side, a turned face frozen
under a concrete canopy, legs bent
toward Mecca. She lowered the tray.
I reached for a date, and my mouth
watered to taste its sugar.

Ameh Joon
AUNT DEAR

My one-breasted, crippled aunt wilts
in her wheelchair, her pale cheeks
and eyes gray, her one breast rolling
into her abdomen like a tear. It seemed
I had just seen her heavy breasts float
to the surface of marbled bathwater,
the soap swirling around two mounds
of flesh. She called me in to tell me
how they pushed a rifle into the folds
of her stomach because she crossed
a city street in Tehran. She floated,
big and naked in the tub, nestled
in a small Manhattan apartment, away
from stinking streets and old religion,
away from the traffic of Queens.

She always had her plate of food,
every night the same. Grandpa always
made sure she was fed and covered.
Mother tells stories of how she ran
to her house when she was a girl,
to hide behind her bedstand and stare
into the beaded turquoise in the silver,
stare into the silk weave of the rugs.

She leans on a brittle arm, her ribcage
twisted to a hook, belly sunk, no longer
the fertile round it once was. Lines
run hard from her nose to her chin,
her wrinkled hands lie like knots
on the silver handles, and she reminds
me in a broken voice how I offered
to gather flowers for her hair when she
once cried, but I said it wrong in Persian.

I once went running and returned
in a sleeveless leotard, my body full
with womanhood and beaded sweat,
warm and wet, a man on her couch,
her company. And only her eyes
showed from the folds of her chador.
I hear her gasp from under the cloth.
Run and cover yourself! Run! Run!
Run! she said in the stern voice
of a whispering prophet.

Mornings I hear her pull herself along
a wall like old men and women tired
of time, pull herself into the bathroom,
out of the bathroom, over the porcelain
and into the washtub, over the porcelain
and onto the tiles, whispering the prayer
over and over, whispers, whispers,
The Great, The Compassionate,
The Powerful, for pity, for pity.

Kae Meeyai
WHEN WILL YOU VISIT

—for Ameh Nosrat

I didn't know how to pray. I wanted it
anyway and quietly folded her prayer
rug, blue on red, green on white, beads
and stones rattling inside. It wasn't enough
to remember how she prayed, wrapping
her chador around her heavy breasts,
how it hugged her hips like an eager child,
the cloth pulled tight on her round body.
Forgive us if we say she loved you best,
they said. And I wanted the rug.

It wasn't enough to remember her roll
the meat in her greased fingers, plump
with blood, two slits of light for eyes.
I wanted her eyebrows to hook, to hear
her tell her stories, how postars almost took
her in for walking down the wrong street.
A gun in my stomach, she said, and raised
her shiny palms, *Mosh Allah! Mosh Allah!*

I knew when her fingers thinned, frail
and dry, how they brushed across linen,
her skin as white as ice-flowers. I never saw
her high on morphine, circle her yellow head
in sheets, turn her tired eyes to the window,
whispering, *B'esm Allah Rahmoneh Rahim,*
In the name of God, Most Merciful, Gracious,
straining her voice until it had no breath.

I call her back from the Land of Ghosts,
scratch the marble, rub a stone across
each ridge of her name. It wasn't enough
that she was sick and hollow-boned.
Ice-flowers fall from my fists. I turn
from the hard scratches under the flowers,
and stand breathless at the pale, green stone.
I felt her voice, hot from the earth, rise
through white linens and concrete cracks,
Kae Meeyai, azizam, Kae Meeyai.

Fereshteh Street

—for Kholeh Nina

Nina lines her eight pills by her dish
before each meal and moans, Will I
get better soon? Each day the same,
each month the same. The same each
year for forty-four. Her childhood folds
in shades of paper homes and sky. Will
I get better soon? She seems to stand
in the roses like an oversized pear,
the earth beneath her feet as thick
as blood. Say something sweet and nice,
she says, *Paschmak, Rohategholghoon,*
Paschmak, Rohategholghoon. Then
wipe the dirty clean, she says, *Pock-esh*
kon, Wipe it clean, slipping her foot
along the ground, Wipe it clean, gurgling
her voice with age, with rotting sound.

Muslin wound Great-Grandfather's
face, his arms, his knees faced Mecca,
and Nina pulled her words from where
he lay, gave her pain away in picture
books, her words shaking fat at each
turned page. Now she finds her genius
in a torture that visits us all, in leaves
breaking edges down his grave like cliffs.
And snow defines the dark shadows
lost in the wave of his absence.

Midnight walls of Grandmother's
house push shadows, and Nina thinks
she hears Great-Grandfather moan.
Fereshteh Street rings with her screams.
The neighbors say they understand.
And Mother hurls Nina's whirling
at the bed nine times to calm her
for beating her hair, for anger. She'll
find herself again, and full of face.
Won't take her pills today, is tired
of bending her neck to her glass
cabinet, her figurines, of asking
the same question for over forty years.

She's tired of having no husband,
no children, no place to go, of waiting
for yellow mornings to fall to her
like the crested pages of the old
Koran. Prayers unfold from minarets.
And Nina shuffles quiet to her sink,
the same each dawn, to wash her arms
and face for prayer, the bundled rug
tucked under her arm. As if she
were the banished king she loved
who carried to his exile his pouch
of soil. *B'esm Allah Rahmoneh Rahim.*
Her hands shake in and out of prayer
beads, her face, the sky, *Allah hu*
Akbar, Allah hu Akbar, her fingers
filling the hungry space of silence.

Boro!
GET AWAY!

Mother squatted till four that night on the bathroom tile,
blue with more than four months waiting, *Boro!*—Get away!
she said to me, the hallway lit by a door's glow shut
at its end, lit for me by knowing my brother floated
and twisted like autumn moving its red on Saddle River.
Yet I waited for him in the stream of light at the door,
not really knowing any better even when I saw the water
ripple red and thick in the bowl. Her smile was quiet
in the hospital room, the windows clean, busy with traffic
and Manhattan smoke. Father called me down to shake
the doctor's hand who birthed me twelve years before.
But I chose to keep at that window instead. And they
scraped her insides clean in some other white room.

Henduneh! Henduneh!

Outside Grandmother's gate, I hear, *Henduneh! Henduneh!*
The bearded vendor slaps his watermelons as if they were
newborns, his fingernails red from lifting platefuls of *Shah
Toot*. Grandmother's wide stare fills her glass. She gave me
her strong hair, her knotted hands. I watch them gnarl
and root around a cheesecloth bundle she squeezes.
The pink flesh yields its juice to her palms and my glass.
She's never minded swallowing the seeds. I spit them
out. I'm not sure I'm ready for stretching and squeezing
dry. Like Grandmother, like Mother, like the Caspian.
Some villager curls asleep in his wheelbarrow, swimming free.

NIKITA'S GRAVE

                              I've often been told
by my father I once could fit in his palm,
his fingers bent to the rounded weight,
my bottom swelling to the creases of his hand.
I've been told of my sister buried somewhere
in upstate New Jersey, eight years older
than me, named for the daylight crackling
of branches and rain. The doctor measured
Mother's hips too big. No air to the brain.
Nikita's hands moved quick. Then stopped.
Father says he took her away and drove
her alone through highways and trash, to bury
his pain in Jersey humidity. There's no point
in a funeral for an immigrant child just turned
American. How he hurried back to echoes,
walls, hard with a sterile ringing of two days'
labor, a silent space where Mother waited,
quiet and empty, her hands filling her lap.
She was beautiful, he says. And I'm not sure
whom he means as he smiles at the heat
in his hands, filling its folds with shadows
of flushed skin.

I've learned to work
around the empty spaces, watch winter peel
birches inward, see snow settle and thread
branches November spares. I hear muddied
noises of a plot peeling in wet earth where
a proud Iranian immigrant planted his firstborn
daughter, left her dust its place to soak
and brush in water. Only the dying fill
with sounds and words and paint and clay.
Somewhere in Jersey my name is written,
stiff and white.

        It is autumn. The empty
define. There is red beauty in dying from
the edges in. Old leaves unwind, circle,
knit the air, the black roots. I settle along
spaces people weave, petals crotchet black
branches white before they fill with green.

BURIAL

My mother scratched the dust of a foreign city
and planted her pale daughter with irises, kept her
warm with a lilac patch of young pigeons and bird
seeds, no one to tell but the barren woman who
rejoiced downstairs. The devil is better when you
know him, my father would say. It was a reason
to stay, and he cried in the shower, wet and hidden,
because he missed the sun too, the baked walls
of pigeon sanctuaries jutting silver from Isfahan's
brown rolls, the busy murmurs of two hundred hot
bodies nestled in the fat land, alive and quivering.

He knocked and split the gazz, the raspy white
nougat stuck into his floured palms. White dust
spilled and irises rose from wisps in black earth ready
to unfold from the ground like dancers, arms lifted,
white skirts spread and circling. Remember how
sweet it is, he said each time. He uncurled her fists
and told her to throw the wisps away. They sat on
the tattered couch in the attic and heard New York,
the rain beating on the hard rustle of feathers,
a rush of pigeons struggle and slip, shift and settle
on the narrow sills of the brown tenement.

Dreaming of a Dancer

—for Anne

Father dreams the echoes of her dance,
the brush of her pointed toe tracing
half-moons in wooden floors, her knee
curved in as if ready to beat and lift
from a black pool, as if it were a rush
of feathers rising from the safe nest
of a mother's breast. He dreams her,

cold and asleep in the quilt an old man
gave when the car came to rest. To keep
her warm, he says, To keep her warm,
and rain gathers under her eyes, pushing
as if cupped in magnolias, running down
in paths of frayed stitches. Woolen
flowers ripple with moonlight.

∽ IV ∽

How did Joseph's scent come to Jacob?
Huuuuu.

How did Jacob's sight return?
Huuuu.

A little wind cleans the eyes.
Like this.

When Shams comes back from Tabriz,
he'll put just his head around the edge
of the door to surprise us.
Like this.

—RUMI

THAT KIND OF SLEEP

—for Grandfather

A man goes to sleep in the town where he has always lived,
and he dreams he's living in another town. . . .The world is
that kind of sleep. —RUMI

PROLOGUE: FROM THE BEGINNING

It is finished. Only
the stillness of time, of a door still closing
the air in a room, his breathing held
by the sheets where his bedclothes still
spread, into the brass of a belt still hung
from the chair, tongues of shoes still laced
at the door. Grandmother says she'll have it
no other way. And it is so.

I've learned to see
here, the drapes burst up and out with wind,
his bedroom breathes its space to some other
time, some other place. Here his house
breathes deeply with sleep after he brings
his tea to his teeth, after he covers his dreaming
with sheets, he'll tighten the shoes on his feet
when he wakes, when he takes his hat, when
he walks to another place. He'll set this
stillness free.

                    And again
the house breathes deeply with sleep, almost
like the night before, and the night before,
and every night for fifty-four years. There is
no difference between one kind of sleep
and another.
                    He will breathe
a loud sleep, his heels will crack with gold.
And I will have the words pull gently
at his mouth, and he will speak, the rim
of his hat will lift the wind, and I will have him
alive with line and light and sound, if death
is a sudden waking to some other town.

1. Finishing Early

Lili's morning holds
its breath as round and full as turquoise
domes. She took her night for finding
one pistachio shell that wouldn't split
when the nut pulled loose—when the gold
pushed in. When her work is done, Lili
laughs and lifts the nuts on her palms,
lets them run like water. Her feet bare
quick to smuggle the gift she's hidden
to the mail. And it's still dark when she
kneels on her roof and wishes her sister
would travel back home. She would clasp
the gift around her wrist herself, she thinks.
Someone unlocks the gates, and Lili
worries how much gold it takes to rattle
pistachios in a mailman's pouch. Minarets
breathe their darkness out with the first
voices of prayer.

2. In Parsis Palace

Shahnaz turned rubber bands around
her ring finger, threatened to marry
the General's son. The walls echoed
with her father's scolding, the queen's
murmurs of her itchy palms, the money
to come. And forty years ago, the tea
boiled over the samovar.

                    Wires twist
the quiet, banisters lean into a still,
old space, into the small gardener
who says it wasn't always this way.

3. AT THE MOSQUE

Wrinkled women
seem twice as many, their faces ridged
as if plowed, slumped along mirrored
domes, fat and dried like desert crows.
Outside a woman bickers over the price
of wool, her teeth tugging at her black
chador. A dog barks. A dirty child
arches her back and beats her heels
in the fountain where others drink
from cups tied with string. Inside they
whisper and pray, low and hard, Praise
be to God, the cherisher and sustainer
of the world, nodding and swaying
to coins rumbling down the slitted box.

4. Late Breakfast in the Bazaar

Agha Rashid and Agha Shaheen lean tall
bows on crates, kneel to break their bread.
The feta cheese crumbles in their hands
like dried wood, like cotton. They whisper,
Peet Peet Pambey, reminding passersby
they can make their pillows plush, Like
new, For a low fee, Very cheap, Very cheap.
Agha Rashid likes to roll his bread around
cucumbers and cheese, holds it tight as if
it were his wife wrapped in her chador.
He wonders if Lili's pillows flatten,
remembers the day she was born, how they
laid the blankets in the grass and let the sky
lift her palms, how he and his brother
have knocked on every door on every street
for more than sixty years, For a low fee,
Like new. The dervish tips his head as if
invited, kneels beside them, leans his axe
on a bow, and rolls his cheese with mint,
its leaves quivering to the fresh sounds
of a green remembering.

5. Trying to Leave

   Grandfather wore his new
shoes, got the heels slit open at the airport.
They were looking for gold.

6. At Noon

       Nina crouched for hours over
the kabob sizzling on the iron, her arms
and legs bare and round and bent with flesh,
straining the top of an old cardboard box
back and forth to scatter the smoke. She
dreams she'll leave the only village she's
ever slept in, smuggle her rings to Turkey,
past the man breaking sugar on an anvil,
past the young boy screaming *Carafs!*,
past the rabid dog that she's left to die
alone on the side of Pahlavi Street.

7. AT EXACTLY TWO

                    The women bloomed.
They had it planned, waited for the minute
hand, and black chadors downtown dropped
down lipstick, hair, bare shoulders, gowns.
Their heels snapped quick around the falling
cloth like polished nails, their legs shimmered
under the light. Perfumes tucked around
their bending and picking up. Hundreds
unburied, unwrapped, unfolded, uncovered,
until the tanks came pushing through.
No one said they heard or knew.

8. On Mahmoodieh

        Esmat Khanoom noticed
when the beggar stole her change. Streets
ripple like shadows, moving slow with black
banners and sheets for Moharam and Safar.
A mullah fills the sky with his noon cry
from the minaret. Beggars lie on their ears,
tracing their lives in the sand, hearing prayers
uncurl the stones. We bury our dead alive,
They say. Then lift their hands to the jangle
in Esmat's pockets.

9. AT THE PALACE GARDEN

                    Nothing
in the green but an ancient man collecting
the moments of them, his skin braided
down his back, brown and leaning down
his shovel. He whispers verse as if
a heap of earth would hear.

10. PEET PEET PAMBEY

                  Esmat Khanoom
spreads open a window, leans into muffled
noises. Her feet mold bare into the carpet
her family has owned for generations,
the one on which her great-grandmother
was born and her mother was married.
The one on which she crawled, on which
her daughters and granddaughters snapped
and crunched pistachios, laughing,
laughing. She listens, looks, can almost
hear all the voices at once, the shimmering
cries of labor, the mullah's marriage chants,
the scuffs of swelling knees and palms,
the snapping and tearing and swallowing.
It seems the spaces have left their marks
in faded colors too often witness
to their living, the passing time looking
like fresh bread, she thinks.

        Agha Rashid
and Agha Shaheen squat on her porch,
their faces elbow-deep in blankets, pillows.
The metal strings on their bows roll taut
over cotton, ripping the matted lumps,
sounding like *Peet Peet Pambey, Peet Peet
Pambey.*
        Esmat listens. When they
finish, the sewn end of the pillow is plush
and tall, and the air will lift a tuft of white
to Esmat's eyes.

11. A Karaj Boy

His grandmother wrapped him in quilts
she had made from her skirts, sold him
for squash in the city bazaar. Time
would twirl him in ropes and move him
slowly through the desert. His mother
still dreams of pressing her son's red
cheek to her breast. Her arms still bend
his breath to her song, *Don't look for me
—I am in your looking.* Children squat
in a wheelbarrow, selling flowers knotted
together, waiting for their father to lift
the handles and roll them homeward
before the last prayers fall like hard rain.

12. At the Street Corner

              Agha Jamsheed kneels
into the sewage canals with his cratefuls
of fruit, cups fresh water, filling sun-dried
celery, *Most Gracious, Most Merciful,*
Master of the day of Judgement. His stare
pours into tight clusters of grapes, checking
for spiders. His hands rake the cherries
for wood. No sound but the clack and ring
of the metal scales. He thinks of his wife
and the tea, and opens his mouth to yawn.
It is filled with gold.

13. Lili Knows Too Much

Lili knows she'll never leave this place.
She stands at her window waiting to hear
from her sister though she knows the gift
she's sent hasn't reached her yet.
                         A baby
is born in a village a day away, and Lili
knows. She thinks she can hear it cry,
remembers the gold her baby girl wore
thirty years ago and she listens. *Peet Peet
Pambey* whispers next door. She's tired.
She knows, understands the stillness of this
time of day, her arms wet with evening
prayers, a coldness that waits for a sleep
when she won't dream of who she is, when
her world knows no quiet remembering.

14. NANEH JAN SLEEPS

               Naneh Jan drinks
her tea from the saucer. All night she's
ground the meat, pushing cubed flesh,
pulling bloodied strands to her copper
bowl. She's chopped parsley, clean
and green, filling the room with its scent
each time she shaved another layer from
the watering trunks. Grandfather wouldn't
let her sleep inside because he said she
smelled so bad. Her body stale with old
saffron and turmeric, her veins as green
as dill. She would sleep in the flowers,
she said, To stay nearer to God. And set
the long, tough rope of her hair braided red,
black, brown, and silver, unbent herself,
tall in the bed and opened her last decaying
tooth to the sky, I have twelve children,
she said, And when the last of my daughters
is married—then, I can die.

15. What Everyone Does

                              When wind fills
Lili's drapes with darkness, Nina still
looks in her glass figurines for something
to hold, Grandfather turns his face
to Esmat, his wife, asks for tea, sets
his shoes on the third shelf as he has
for fifty years, one heel taller than
the other. Agha Jamsheed makes love
to his wife, his fruit crates empty,
casting shadows in moving stripes
on her breasts. They look like baskets,
he thinks. Lili's sister may receive
a bracelet in a week or two. Agha Rashid
and Agha Shaheen sleep in the grass.
They have no blanket. A mother rocks
her screaming newborn to her breast.
Naneh Jan stirs. Grandfather lowers
the steaming cup from his teeth, pulls
his bed sheets over his shoulders, over
his ears for quieter dreams.

16. CARRYING HOME

The dervish on Fereshteh Street loves
to be one with the universe. He drops
to the earth and buries his face in the dust
because he loves to be photographed.
His skin burns as red and dry as the Alborz
mountains. The city whirls his silver hair
and beard, spinning Rumi to the alley,

> *We are the night ocean filled*
> *with glints of light. We are the space*
> *between the fish and the moon,*
> *while we sit here together.*

                         Words
move in and from the shadows. And when
he is quiet, he hears his mountains call
him home. His pouch sways full with tools,
the crescent blade of his axe hangs like
the moon from his shoulders, a small
light at the end of the street flickers out
and the alley is black and silent but for
the clink of his heels, loud with moonlight.

Glossary

Allah hu Akbar	"God is great," part of the Muslim daily prayers
Ameh	paternal aunt
Arouss	bride
Attar	name meaning "fire"; name of an angel
Avenue Vali Asr	a major avenue in Tehran
Azizam	my dear
Bakhlava	a Persian / Mediterranean pastry
Barikalla	bravo
Bazaar	the market place
B'esm Allah Rahmoneh Rahim	In the name of God, Most Merciful, Most Gracious
Boro	go
Boro ounja	go / get over there
Carafs	celery
Caspian	the Caspian Sea borders Iran along the northern border

Chador..a long cloth with which Islamic women cover their hair and bodies

Chetel Setoun ....forty columns

Doukgh...a drink made with water, yoghurt, salt, and mint

Dervish ....Persian term, derived from *dar* or "door." One who goes from door to door. Also, one who is at the threshold (with awareness between this world and the Divine).

Esmat ....name meaning "honesty" or "greatness / goodness"

Fariba...name meaning "charming, enticing"

Fereshteh..name of a street; literally means "angel"

Gazz...a hard white nougat candy with pistachio nuts or almonds kept in flour; it is difficult and messy to break and eat

Hafiz...Persian mystical poet

Henduneh ....watermelon

Henna...an herbal hair dye, which can be black, red, or neutral

Isfahan ....a historical town south of Tehran, the capital of Iran

Jamsheed ....name from *Shahnameh* or *Book of Kings;* an ancient Persian King

Jan / Joon ....dear

Kabob .... grilled meat

Kae Meeyai .... "when will you visit?"

Karaj .... a city west of Tehran

Khayyám .... Eleventh-century Persian poet and
mathematician

Kholeh .... maternal aunt

Kohl .... a soft black cosmetic
eye-pencil

Koran .... the Muslim holy book

Land of the Ghosts .... literally translated from the Farsi
and is where dead people are
believed to reside

Lili .... name meaning "a flower"

Mahmoodieh .... name of a street; "Mahmood" means
"praised"

Marvari .... pearls

Mecca .... the holy city of Islam

Moharam .... Shiite lunar mourning month,
mourning the Karbala tragedy when
Imam Houssein, grandson of
Prophet Muhammed, was martyred
in the early days of Islamic history

Mosh Allah .... "my God"

Mount Arafat .... the mountain to which pilgrims
travel to throw stones at the Pillar
of Shayton for symbolic cleansing

Mullah .... an Islamic cleric

Na Cun.."don't do that"

Naneh...Nanny or Governess; literal transla-
tion of the old style or traditional
name for Mother

Nina...name meaning "grace of God"

Obb..water

Pock-esh kon...................................."erase it"

Pahlavi...name of a street; named after the
family name of the late Shah, King
of Iran

Parsis...Zoroastrian Persians

Paschmak..cotton candy

Peet Peet Pambey..............................onomatopoeia; the sound made by
the instrument used to fluff the
filling of pillows and comforters.
"Pambey" means "cotton"

Porr Rou...literally translated as "full
of face," meaning feisty, full
of attitude, or having "nerve"

Postar...revolutionary guard

Rashid..name meaning "brave"

Rohategholghoon..............................jelly candy

Rumi..Persian mystical poet

Sadi...Persian mystical poet

Safar..the month following Moharam

Samovar .... a large silver pot which boils water for tea

Shah Toot .... berry resembling a giant raspberry; literally means "King of berries"

Shaheen .... name meaning "falcon"

Shayton .... Satan

Soheila .... name meaning "star"

Tehran .... the capital of Iran

Terrmeh .... a hand-woven, hand-embroidered fabric used only on special occasions (for important prayers, at the wedding altar, or as a funeral dressing, etc.)

Vali Asr .... name of an avenue; literally means "messiah"

Zohreh .... name meaning "planet Venus" or "love, harmony, devotion"

SUSAN ATEFAT-PECKHAM writes poetry and creative nonfiction, and is a musician and an abstract expressionist painter. Her work is informed by many countries. She was born first-generation American to Iranian parents, and has lived most of her life in France and Switzerland although she has also lived in the United States and Iran. She earned her Ph.D. from the University of Nebraska-Lincoln, where she taught creative writing, literature, and composition, and was an editorial assistant for *Prairie Schooner*. Her nonfiction manuscript, *Black Eyed Bird*, finished in the final rounds of judging for the Associated Writing Programs Intro Award and was Runner-Up in the Beryl Markham Award for Creative Nonfiction (Story Line Press). Her work has been selected for inclusion in the anthology, *Common Ground: An Anthology of Multi-cultural Writing* (Prentice-Hall), and new work has appeared or is forthcoming in *Borderlands— Texas Poetry Review*, *The International Poetry Review*, *International Quarterly*, *The Literary Review*, *The MacGuffin*, *Northwest Review*, *Onthebus*, *Prairie Schooner*, *Puerto Del Sol*, *The Southern Poetry Review*, *The Sycamore Review*, *The Texas Review*, and *Under the Sun*. She is currently Assistant Professor of Creative Writing at Hope College in Holland, Michigan, where she lives with her husband and two small sons.

THE COFFEE HOUSE of seventeenth-century England was a place of fellowship where ideas could be freely exchanged. The coffee house of 1950s America was a place of refuge and of tremendous literary energy. At the turn of our latest century, coffee house culture abounds at corner shops and on-line. We hope this spirit welcomes our readers into the pages of Coffee House Press books.

POETRY TITLES FROM COFFEE HOUSE PRESS

Cantos to Blood and Honey by Adrian Castro
The Green Lake Is Awake by Joseph Ceravolo
Easter Sunday by Tom Clark
87 North by Michael Coffey
Panoramas by Victor Hernández Cruz
Red Beans by Victor Hernández Cruz
Madame Deluxe by Tenaya Darlington
Routine Disruptions by Kenward Elmslie
Decoy by Elaine Equi
Surface Tension by Elaine Equi
Voice-Over by Elaine Equi
Shiny Pencils at the Edge of Things by Dick Gallup
Dog Road Woman by Allison Coke Hedge
The Book of Medicines by Linda Hogan
Savings by Linda Hogan
Corvus by Anselm Hollo
Outlying Districts by Anselm Hollo
Pick Up the House by Anselm Hollo
Drawing the Line by Lawson Fusao Inada
Legends from Camp by Lawson Fusao Inada
Teducation by Ted Joans
Unlocking the Exits by Eliot Katz
Cranial Guitar by Bob Kaufman
Cant Be Wrong by Michael Lally
Paul Metcalf: Collected Works, Volume I, 1956 – 1976
Paul Metcalf: Collected Works, Volume II, 1976 – 1986
Paul Metcalf: Collected Works, Volume III, 1987 – 1997
Margaret & Dusty by Alice Notley
Revenants by Mark Nowak
Sacred Vows by Sam U Oeur
Great Balls of Fire by Ron Padgett
Of Flesh & Spirit by Wang Ping
Thirsting for Peace in a Raging Century by Edward Sanders
Clinch by Michael Scholnick
Earliest Worlds by Eleni Sikelianos
Avalanche by Quincy Troupe
Choruses by Quincy Troupe
Breakers by Paul Violi
Helping the Dreamer by Anne Waldman
Iovis: All Is Full of Jove by Anne Waldman
Iovis Book II by Anne Waldman
Vow to Poetry by Anne Waldman
Nice to See You: Homage to Ted Berrigan Anne Waldman, editor
The Annotated "Here" by Marjorie Welish

Available at fine bookstores everywhere.
Good books are brewing at coffeehousepress.org

COLOPHON

That Kind of Sleep was designed at Coffee House Press
in the Warehouse District of downtown Minneapolis.
The text is set in Caslon.